P9-CQJ-491

PULLEYS

by Sally M. Walker and Roseann Feldmann
photographs by Andy King

Lerner Publications Company • Minneapolis

For my daughter, Chrissie, love you forever—RF

The publisher wishes to thank the Minneapolis Kids program for its help in the preparation of this book.

Additional photographs are reproduced with permission from: © Kevin Schafer / Corbis, p. 30; © James P. Blair / Corbis, p. 38; © M. Bryan Ginsberg, p. 43.

Text copyright © 2002 by Sally M. Walker and Roseann Feldmann
Photographs copyright © 2002 by Andy King

Lerner Publications Company
A division of Lerner Publishing Group
241 First Avenue North
Minneapolis, MN 55401 U.S.A.

Website address: www.lernerbooks.com

Library of Congress Cataloging-in-Publication Data

Walker, Sally M.
  Pulleys / by Sally M. Walker and Roseann Feldmann ; photographs by Andy King.
     p.   cm. — (Early bird physics books)
  Includes index.
  ISBN 0-8225-2220-9 (lib. bdg. : alk. paper)
  1. Pulleys—Juvenile literature. [1. Pulleys.] I. Feldmann, Roseann. II. King, Andy, ill.
III. Title. IV. Series.
TJ1103 .W35 2002
621.8'11—dc21   00-011961

Manufactured in the United States of America
1 2 3 4 5 6 – JR – 07 06 05 04 03 02

CONTENTS

BE A WORD DETECTIVE

Can you find these words as you read about pulleys?
Be a detective and try to figure out what they mean.
You can turn to the glossary on page 46 for help.

complicated machines
compound pulley
fixed pulley
force
friction
gravity

load
moveable pulley
pulley
simple machines
work

Eating an apple is work. What does the word "work" mean to a scientist?

Chapter 1

WORK

You work every day. When you raise window blinds, you are working. Playing and eating snacks are work, too!

When scientists use the word "work," they don't mean the opposite of play. Work is using a force to move an object. Force is a push or a pull. You use force to play, to eat, and to do chores.

You work when you play cards!

These kids are moving sand from one place to another place. They are doing work.

Every time your force moves an object, you have done work. It does not matter how far the object moves. If it moves, work has been done.

If the object has not moved, you have not done work. It does not matter how hard you tried.

This boy is pushing on a house as hard as he can.
But he can't move the house. So he is not doing work.

Cranes are machines that have many moving parts. What do we call machines that have many moving parts?

Chapter 2
MACHINES

Most people want their work to be easy. Machines are tools that make it easier to do work. Some machines make work go faster, too.

Some machines have many moving parts. These machines are called complicated machines. Cranes and cars are complicated machines.

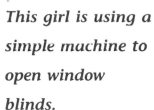

This girl is using a simple machine to open window blinds.

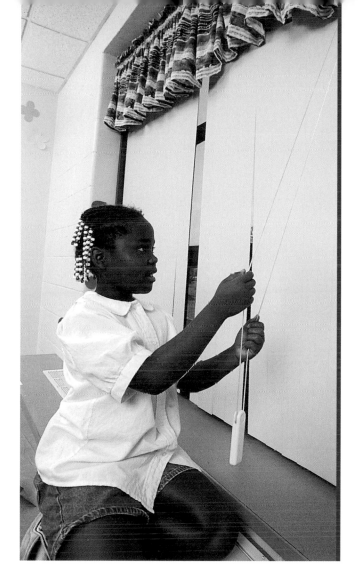

Some machines have few moving parts. These machines are called simple machines. Simple machines are found in every home, school, and playground. They are so simple that most people do not realize they are machines.

Lifting a heavy box is hard work. Why is it easier to lower the box to the ground?

Chapter 3

GRAVITY

Simple machines make your work easier. Some simple machines do this by changing the direction of your force. Pulling upward is hard work. Pulling downward is much easier. It is easier because gravity helps you. Gravity is the force that pulls everything toward the earth.

Some simple machines change an upward force into a downward force. These machines make your work much easier.

When you drop a book, gravity pulls it to the floor. The book stays there until a stronger force moves it.

Gravity is pulling this book toward the floor.

Gravity makes lifting a heavy book hard work.

Put a heavy book on the floor. Now lift it onto a table. Lifting the book is hard work. You must use a lot of force. Your lifting force has to be stronger than the pull of gravity.

Put the book back on the floor. It is much easier to lower the book than to lift it. When you lower the book, gravity helps you.

If your force is in the same direction as gravity, your work is easier. You can prove this. You will need a screwdriver, an empty pop-top can, some small stones or sand, a big paper clip, and a piece of string that is 4 feet long.

You can use these objects to experiment with gravity.

Lift the ring on the can, but don't break it off. Then fill the can with stones.

Bend the ring on the can until it sticks straight up. Fill the can with stones or sand. Next, hook the paper clip on the ring. Tie a loop at one end of the string. The loop should

16

be big enough to fit loosely around your hand.
Hook the loop of string onto the paper clip.
Now put the can on the floor. Hold the string.
Pull up on the string to lift the can onto the
table. You must use a lot of force to lift the can.
How much force must you use?

Hold the string and lift the can up onto the table.

This can is just like yours. It is hanging from a spring scale.
A spring scale measures force. This spring scale is measuring
the force the girl uses to lift the can. She uses about 6 units of
force to lift the can.

18

Now put your screwdriver on the table. Place it so the handle is on the table. The narrow shaft should hang over the edge of the table. Have a friend hold the handle of the screwdriver so it cannot move. Put the can on the floor under the screwdriver.

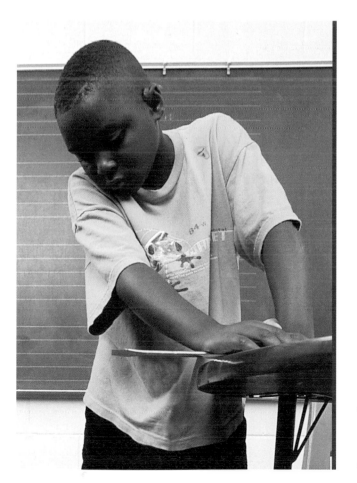

The shaft of your screwdriver should hang over the edge of the table.

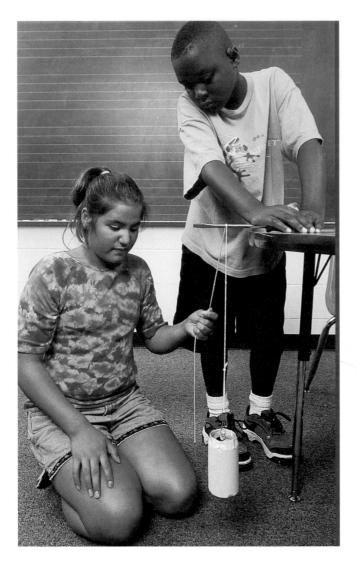

When you pull down on the string, you are pulling with gravity.

Loop the string over the shaft of the screwdriver. When you pull down on the string, the can goes up. The can moves the same distance as it did when you pulled straight up.

But now your arm is pulling with gravity.
Pulling with gravity makes your work easier.

It takes about 6 units of force to lift the can. The force is the same as it was when the other girl lifted the can straight up. But this girl's work is easier because she is pulling down with gravity.

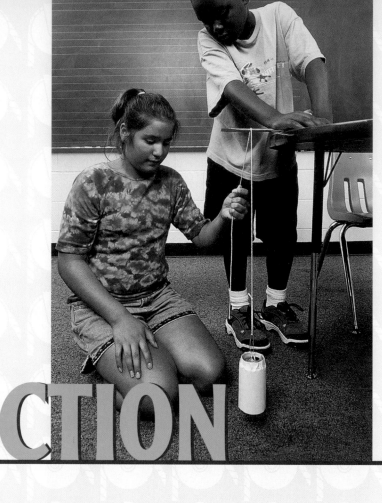

Chapter 4

FRICTION

Raise and lower the can a few times. Notice how the string rubs against the shaft of the screwdriver. The rubbing between the string and the shaft makes friction. Friction is a force that slows or stops moving objects. Friction makes your can move more slowly. If there were less friction, your can would rise faster.

If you raise and lower the can many times, the string will start to wear out. Friction makes the string wear out.

Friction makes it hard to slide a heavy box on a sidewalk.

If there is less friction, the string will not wear out as quickly. How can you make less friction between the screwdriver and the string? Adding a wheel that spins is a great way to make less friction. You can make a spinning wheel with a spool and a rubber band.

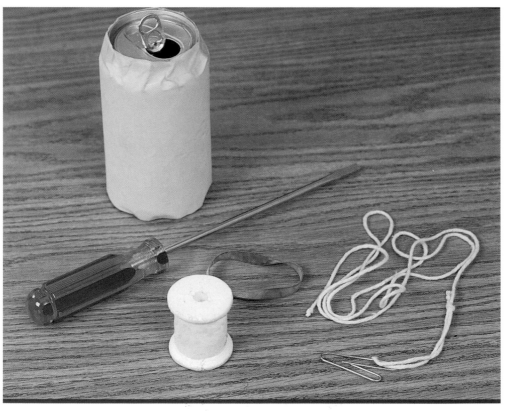

You can use these objects to experiment with spinning wheels.

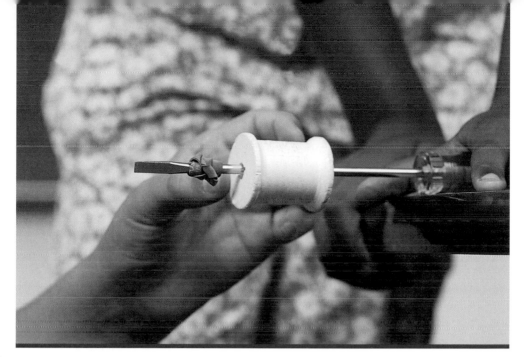

Make sure the spool spins easily on the shaft of the screwdriver.

Slide the spool onto the shaft of your screwdriver. Wrap the rubber band around the tip of the screwdriver. This will keep the spool from sliding off. The spool is now a wheel. It is called a grooved wheel because the ridge at each side makes a groove around the middle. The wheel spins easily around the screwdriver. It spins easily because there is only a little friction between the spool and the screwdriver.

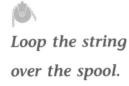

Loop the string over the spool.

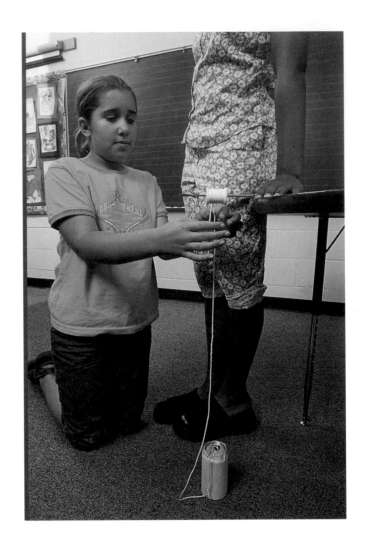

Put the screwdriver back on the table. Have a friend hold it in place. The shaft and the wheel should hang over the edge of the table. Put the can on the floor under the screwdriver. This time, loop the string over the wheel.

Pull down on the string. The wheel and the string both move. There is very little friction. The can moves up really fast. Since the wheel and the string both move, the string rubs less. It will not wear out quickly.

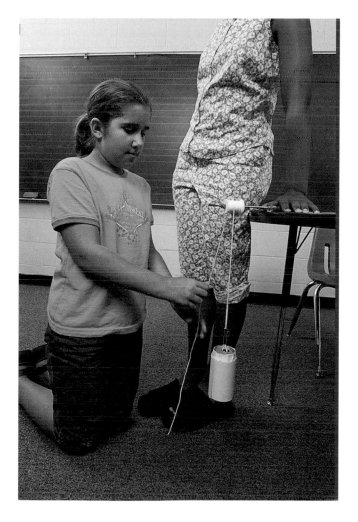

The spool keeps the string from rubbing against the screwdriver.

You have made a simple machine called a pulley! What kind of pulley did you make?

Chapter 5

KINDS OF PULLEYS

When you looped the string over the wheel, you made a pulley. A pulley is a simple machine. One end of your pulley's string is fastened to the can full of stones. The can is your pulley's load. A load is an object you want to move. The wheel of your pulley is grooved. The groove keeps the string from slipping off the wheel.

The pulley you made is called a fixed pulley. A fixed pulley stays attached in one place. It does not move.

A flagpole has a fixed pulley at the top. The flag is attached to a rope. The rope runs over the pulley. You pull down on one end of the rope. The flag goes up the pole. Using a fixed pulley to raise the flag makes your work easy.

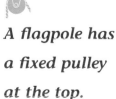

A flagpole has a fixed pulley at the top.

29

Another kind of pulley is called a moveable pulley. A moveable pulley does not stay in one place. A moveable pulley is attached to a load. When the load moves, the pulley moves too. You use less force when you use a moveable pulley than when you use a fixed pulley. Using less force makes your work easier.

This girl is holding on to a moveable pulley. The pulley moves with her as she rides along the wire.

You can make a moveable pulley with a sewing machine spool called a bobbin, two big paper clips, a straw, and the can and the string you used before.

A bobbin is a grooved wheel. Slide the bobbin onto the straw. Make sure the bobbin spins easily around the straw.

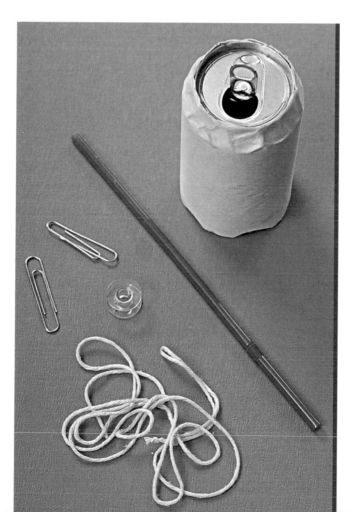

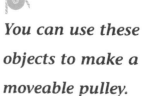

You can use these objects to make a moveable pulley.

Hook both paper clips to the ring on your can. Slip one paper clip onto one end of the straw. Slip the other paper clip onto the other end of the straw. The bobbin will be between the two paper clips.

Wrap a piece of tape around each end of the straw. The tape will keep the bobbin and the paper clips from slipping off.

There is a loop at the end of your string. Put the loop over a doorknob. Put the other end of the string around your bobbin. The bobbin is now a moveable pulley. Gently pull up on the string. Pull until the string begins to lift the pulley and the can.

Pull up on the string to lift the load.

Raise the end of the string up to the doorknob. See how the pulley rolls along the string. As the moveable pulley moves, the load moves too. It's easy to lift the load with your moveable pulley.

The pulley and the load move together in a moveable pulley.

34

Remember when you lifted the load with your fixed pulley? You used about 6 units of force to lift the load.

Think about your earlier lifts. First, you lifted the can straight up. Then you pulled down when you used your fixed pulley. The fixed pulley is the one that your friend held in place. Both times the load was hooked to one end of the string. You pulled on the other end. When you pulled, the load moved up. Both times you lifted the whole weight of the load yourself. You used a lot of force to do that.

You use less force to pull upward with your moveable pulley than to pull downward with your fixed pulley. Why do you need to use less force with the moveable pulley?

You use less force with your moveable pulley. This girl is using about 3 units of force to lift the load.

Look again at your moveable pulley. The can is not hooked to the end of the string. The end of the string is attached to the doorknob. Lift the load again. You are not holding the whole load yourself. What else is helping you hold the load? The doorknob is helping you. You use less force because the doorknob holds some of the load's weight. Lifting less weight makes your work easier.

These are compound pulleys. A compound pulley is also called a block and tackle.

You can make your work even easier if you use a compound pulley. A compound pulley is two or more pulleys working together. You can make a compound pulley. You just need to add a fixed pulley to your moveable pulley.

You made a fixed pulley before. It is the screwdriver with the spool on it. Put the shaft of the screwdriver on the doorknob. Have a friend hold both ends of the screwdriver in place.

Hold the screwdriver in place on the doorknob.

Raise and lower your load. Is it easy?

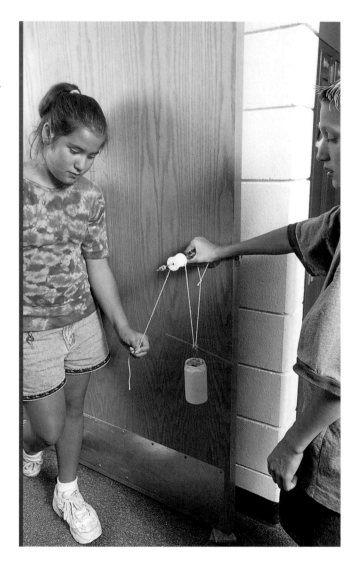

Put the string around the moveable pulley. Then put the loose end of the string over the fixed pulley. It is very easy to raise and lower the load. The fixed pulley lets you pull downward with gravity. And the moveable pulley makes the doorknob hold part of the weight of the load.

You are still using about 3 units of force to lift the load. But the compound pulley makes your work easier because you are pulling down with gravity.

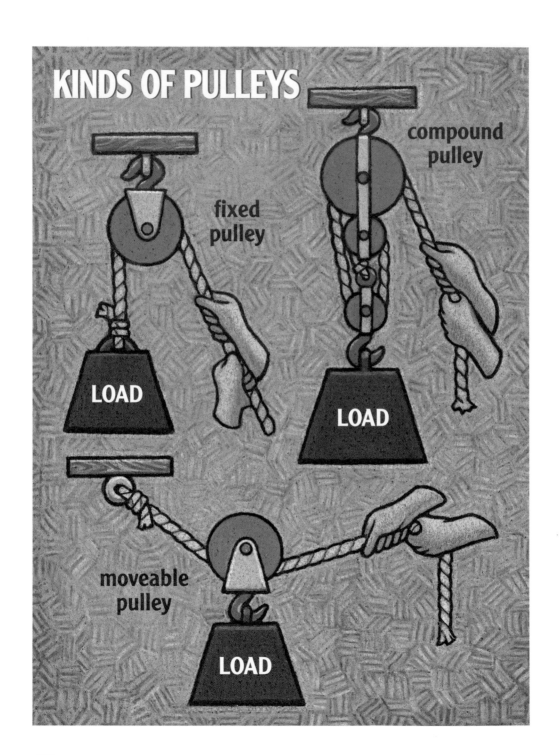

KINDS OF PULLEYS

compound pulley

fixed pulley

LOAD

LOAD

moveable pulley

LOAD

You have learned a lot about pulleys. Some pulleys change the direction of your force. Some pulleys let you use less force.

Using a pulley gives you an advantage. An advantage is a better chance of finishing your work. Using a pulley is almost like having a helper. That makes your work easier. And that is a real advantage.

This clothesline has a fixed pulley at each end.
The pulleys are both attached to the building.

ON SHARING A BOOK

When you share a book with a child, you show that reading is important. To get the most out of the experience, read in a comfortable, quiet place. Turn off the television and limit other distractions, such as telephone calls. Be prepared to start slowly. Take turns reading parts of this book. Stop occasionally and discuss what you're reading. Talk about the photographs. If the child begins to lose interest, stop reading. When you pick up the book again, revisit the parts you have already read.

Be a Vocabulary Detective

The word list on page 5 contains words that are important in understanding the topic of this book. Be word detectives and search for the words as you read the book together. Talk about what the words mean and how they are used in the sentence. Do any of these words have more than one meaning? You will find the words defined in a glossary on page 46.

What about Questions?

Use questions to make sure the child understands the information in this book. Here are some suggestions:

> What did this paragraph tell us? What does this picture show? What do you think we'll learn about next? What is force? How are simple machines different from complicated machines? What kind of force pulls objects to the ground? What kind of force slows or stops moving objects? How do pulleys help people? How many kinds of pulleys are there? What is your favorite part of the book? Why?

If the child has questions, don't hesitate to respond with questions of your own, such as: What do *you* think? Why? What is it that you don't know? If the child can't remember certain facts, turn to the index.

Introducing the Index

The index helps readers find information without searching through the whole book. Turn to the index on page 47. Choose an entry such as *gravity* and ask the child to use the index to find out if pulling with gravity makes work easier. Repeat with as many entries as you like. Ask the child to point out the differences between an index and a glossary. (The index helps readers find information, while the glossary tells readers what words mean.)

SIMPLE MACHINES

Books

Baker, Wendy, and Andrew Haslam. *Machines*. New York: Two-Can Publishing Ltd., 1993. This book offers many fun educational activities that explore simple machines.

Burnie, David. *Machines: How They Work*. New York: Dorling Kindersley, 1994. Beginning with descriptions of simple machines, Burnie goes on to explore complicated machines and how they work.

Hodge, Deborah. *Simple Machines*. Toronto: Kids Can Press Ltd., 1998. This collection of experiments shows readers how to build their own simple machines using household items.

Van Cleave, Janice. *Janice Van Cleave's Machines: Mind-boggling Experiments You Can Turn into Science Fair Projects*. New York: John Wiley & Sons, Inc., 1993. Van Cleave encourages readers to use experiments to explore how simple machines make doing work easier.

Ward, Alan. *Machines at Work*. New York: Franklin Watts, 1993. This book describes simple machines and introduces the concept of compound machines. Many helpful experiments are included.

Woods, Michael, and Mary B. Woods. *Ancient Machines*. Minneapolis: Runestone Press, 2000. Through photographs and in-depth explanation, this book explores the invention of all six simple machines by various ancient civilizations. It also shows how these machines are the basis of all complicated machines.

Websites

Simple Machines
<http://sln.fi.edu/qa97/spotlight3/spotlight3.html> With brief information about all six simple machines, this site provides helpful links related to each and features experiments for some of them.

Simple Machines—Basic Quiz
<http://www.quia.com/tq/101964.html> This challenging interactive quiz allows budding physicists to test their knowledge of work and simple machines.

GLOSSARY

complicated machines: machines that have many moving parts

compound pulley: two or more pulleys working together

fixed pulley: a pulley that stays attached in one place

force: a push or a pull

friction: a force caused when two objects rub together

gravity: the force that pulls everything toward the earth

load: an object you want to move

moveable pulley: a pulley that is attached to a load

pulley: a wheel that has a rope looped around it. The rope fits in a groove that runs around the edge of the wheel.

simple machines: machines that have few moving parts

work: moving an object from one place to another

INDEX

Pages listed in **bold** type refer to photographs.

About the Authors

Sally M. Walker is the author of many books for young readers. When she isn't busy writing and doing research for books, Ms. Walker works as a children's literature consultant. She has taught children's literature at Northern Illinois University and has given presentations at many reading conferences. She lives in Illinois with her husband and two children.

Roseann Feldmann earned her B.A. degree in biology, chemistry, and education at the College of St. Francis and her M.S. in education from Northern Illinois University. As an educator, she has been a classroom teacher, college instructor, curriculum author, and administrator. She currently lives on six tree-filled acres in Illinois with her husband and two children.

About the Photographer

Freelance photographer Andy King lives in St. Paul, Minnesota, with his wife and daughter. Andy has done editorial photography, including several works for Lerner Publishing Group. Andy has also done commercial photography. In his free time, he plays basketball, rides his mountain bike, and takes pictures of his daughter.

METRIC CONVERSIONS

WHEN YOU KNOW:	MULTIPLY BY:	TO FIND:
miles	1.609	kilometers
feet	0.3048	meters
inches	2.54	centimeters
gallons	3.787	liters
tons	0.907	metric tons
pounds	0.454	kilograms